21st Century Junior Library

COMMUNICATING WITH OTHERS

Building My Social-Emotional Toolbox

Emily Rose

Published in the United States of America by:

CHERRY LAKE PRESS
2395 South Huron Parkway, Suite 200, Ann Arbor, Michigan 48104
www.cherrylakepress.com

Reading Adviser: Beth Walker Gambro, MS, Ed., Reading Consultant, Yorkville, IL

Photo Credits: © Monkey Business Images/Shutterstock.com, cover, 1; © LightField Studios/Shutterstock.com, 5; © GUNDAM_Ai/Shutterstock.com, 6; © Krakenimages.com/Shutterstock.com, 7, 13 [right]; © Sergey Novikov/Shutterstock.com, 8 [left]; © Prostock-studio/Shutterstock.com, 8 [right]; © Vladislav Pavovich/Shutterstock.com, 9; © Littlekidmoment/Shutterstock.com, 10, 11; © Robert Kneschke/Shutterstock.com, 12; © Gena73/Shutterstock.com, 13 [left]; © fizkes/Shutterstock.com, 14; © Chayantorn Tongmorn/Shutterstock.com, 17; © Anna Nahabed/Shutterstock.com, 18; © FoxyImage/Shutterstock.com, 19; © wavebreakmedia/Shutterstock.com, 21; © Honza Hruby/Shutterstock.com, 21 [bottom]

Copyright © 2023 by Cherry Lake Publishing Group

All rights reserved. No part of this book may be reproduced or utilized in any form or by any means without written permission from the publisher.

Cherry Lake Press is an imprint of Cherry Lake Publishing Group.

Library of Congress Cataloging-in-Publication Data

Names: Rose, Emily (School psychologist), author.
Title: Communicating with others / by Emily Rose.
Description: Ann Arbor, Michigan : Cherry Lake Publishing, 2022. | Series: Building my social-emotional toolbox | Includes bibliographical references. | Audience: Grades 2-3
Identifiers: LCCN 2022005343 | ISBN 9781668909041 (hardcover) | ISBN 9781668910641 (paperback) | ISBN 9781668912232 (ebook) | ISBN 9781668913826 (pdf)
Subjects: LCSH: Interpersonal communication in children—Juvenile literature. | Interpersonal relations in children—Juvenile literature.
Classification: LCC BF723.C57 R67 2022 | DDC 155.4/136—dc23/eng/20220214
LC record available at https://lccn.loc.gov/2022005343

Cherry Lake Press would like to acknowledge the work of the Partnership for 21st Century Learning, a Network of Battelle for Kids. Please visit http://www.battelleforkids.org/networks/p21 for more information.

Printed in the United States of America
Corporate Graphics

CONTENTS

There Are Many Ways
to Communicate   4

What Is Communication,
Anyway?   10

What to Do When
Communication Goes Wrong   15

    Extend Your Learning   20
    Glossary   22
    Find Out More   23
    Index   24
    About the Author   24

THERE ARE MANY WAYS TO COMMUNICATE

There are many ways to **communicate** with others. You can communicate by talking, by writing a note, or even with your behavior. Did you know you can communicate without even talking? It's true! Giving someone a flower can communicate, "I care about you," and gritting your teeth or

Did you know that there are more ways to communicate than just talking?

stomping your feet might tell others, "I am mad." Those are examples of **nonverbal** communication, or ways that you communicate your feelings without words by *showing* your feelings instead.

At recess, James got mad at his best friend, Ray, when Ray didn't want to play the game that James wanted to play.

What other ways might people communicate "I am mad" without using their words?

Think!

Give an example of one way you communicated something today. Did you use your voice or your behaviors, write a note, or something else entirely?

James stomped away and didn't talk to Ray for the rest of recess, which hurt Ray's feelings. James wanted to **apologize**, but he didn't know exactly what to say.

That night, James talked to his dad. "Dad, I feel bad for hurting Ray's feelings at school today, but I can't find the words to tell him I'm sorry and make it right. What should I do?"

James's dad gave him a great idea. "Sometimes words can be hard, but there are lots of ways to communicate to Ray that you are sorry. Maybe write him a card explaining your feelings and put it on his desk at school. You could also offer to play a game that he wants to play next time so he'll see that you care about him."

Create!

Practice communicating to someone by writing them a nice note.

How else might you communicate "I'm sorry" to a friend?

WHAT IS COMMUNICATION, ANYWAY?

Communicating means that two or more people are sharing ideas and learning things about each other. Think about it—sharing ideas and stories with other people is the best way to learn new things! If your friend went to space camp for a week, you could learn so many interesting things by asking them to tell you all about it. How cool is that?

Ask Questions!

Next time you are talking to someone, think of a question you could ask that person to keep the **conversation** going and learn something from them!

Looking at someone while they are talking can also communicate "I am listening."

When you are talking to someone, it's important to take turns and spend time listening to the other person too. That way, you can hear what they have to say and maybe even add to what they shared. If you're not listening, you can't learn.

Make a Guess!

If one person talks the whole time and doesn't pause for their friend to share too, how do you think their friend might feel?

For example, Rico got a new bike over the summer break. When school started again, it was all he talked about. He told his friends about the cherry red paint color, the horn on the handlebars, and even the extra-tall tires. When Rico's teacher asked him what his friends at his table had done over the break, Rico realized that he had no idea.

"Oh, no!" said Rico, feeling shocked and **embarrassed**. "I was so excited to talk about my new bike that I didn't even ask my friends what they did this summer!"

When someone doesn't understand what we are trying to communicate, it can be frustrating.

14

WHAT TO DO WHEN COMMUNICATION GOES WRONG

One important thing to know is that some people don't like to talk a lot. Others like to talk all the time. If someone talks more or less than you, that's okay. They might be shy or they might not be interested in talking about the same things as you.

It's also good to remember that sometimes people disagree or misunderstand each other. It happens! It's good to talk to the other person if you feel like you didn't understand something they said or if you sense they didn't understand something you said. That way, you can **resolve** it.

Fatima *loves* dinosaurs. Her favorite is the **triceratops**. Whenever she gets a free minute, she likes to tell everyone cool facts about these **prehistoric** creatures. Then one day in science class, another student at her table yelled, "Nobody *cares* about dinosaurs!" Fatima felt sad, but when class ended, another student came up to her and said,

Look!

Pay attention this week to the ways people around you communicate. Do they talk to each other or write notes to their friends? Or do they communicate with their behaviors?

"I love dinosaurs too!" Fatima realized that talking about dinosaurs with people who weren't interested in them was probably boring for them, but finding someone who likes the same things is way more fun for her *and* her new friend.

It can be easier to talk about something you enjoy with someone who has the same interests.

Communication is important to help us understand others and to be understood too!

The more you think about all the ways you communicate every day, the more you will begin to understand yourself and others.

EXTEND YOUR LEARNING

Remember how some people might like to talk all the time, but others might not like to talk very much? Think about how you feel most comfortable communicating. Once you figure out how you prefer to communicate, how can you use this knowledge in the future?

For example, some people like to write things down because sometimes it feels hard or scary to say them out loud. Whenever they feel a big **emotion** like sadness or fear, they write it down instead of talking about it. That makes them feel better.

GLOSSARY

apologize (uh-PAH-luh-jyze) to say you are sorry for something

communicate (kuh-MYOO-nuh-kayt) to share information, thoughts, or feelings

conversation (kahn-vuhr-SAY-shuhn) a talk between two or more people

embarrassed (im-BARE-uhst) feeling ashamed or self-conscious

emotion (ih-MOH-shuhn) a strong feeling such as love, fear, happiness, or anger

nonverbal (nahn-VUHR-buhl) not spoken

prehistoric (pree-hih-STOR-ik) the time before humans started recording history

resolve (rih-ZAHLV) to come to a conclusion or understanding about something

triceratops (try-SEHR-uh-tahps) a dinosaur with two large horns over its eyes and a smaller horn on its nose

FIND OUT MORE

Books

Murphy, Frank. *Stand Up for Respect.* Ann Arbor, MI: Cherry Lake Publishing, 2019.

Rose, Emily. *Feeling and Showing Empathy.* Ann Arbor, MI: Cherry Lake Publishing, 2022.

Rose, Emily. *Making and Keeping Friends.* Ann Arbor, MI: Cherry Lake Publishing, 2022.

Websites

YouTube—Communication Skills: Empathetic Listening—Inside Out, 2015
https://www.youtube.com/watch?v=t685WM5R6aM
Watch this clip from Pixar's *Inside Out* to see an example of empathetic listening.

YouTube—How Miscommunication Happens (And How to Avoid It)
https://www.youtube.com/watch?v=gCfzeONu3Mo
Watch this video to learn how to avoid miscommunication.

INDEX

apologies, 7–9
asking questions, 11

body language, 4–7

communication
  problems, and
    improvement, 15–19
  sharing and learning, 10–11
communication methods,
    4–5
  nonverbal, 4–7
  preferences, 15, 20
  verbal, 10–13
  writing, 9, 20

conversations and talking
  habits and preferences,
    15–16, 20
  learning, 10–11
  listening, 12–13
  manners, 11–13, 16–17
  understanding, 14–19

emotions, 4–9, 20

feelings, 4–9, 20

interests, 16–17

learning, 10–11, 20
listening, 12–13

misunderstandings, 15–16

nonverbal communication,
    4–7

personalities, 15, 20

question-asking, 11

saying "sorry," 7–9

talking. *See* conversations
  and talking

understanding, 14–19

written communication
  apologies, 9
  preferences, 20

ABOUT THE AUTHOR

Emily Rose is a school psychologist, yoga teacher, and writer for her mental wellness blog, MissMagnoliaSays.com. She enjoys helping kids and adults understand and manage their emotions and live beautiful lives. Emily lives in Dearborn, Michigan.